PRINCETON STUDIES IN INTERNATIONAL FINANCE

No. 80, April 1996

FOREIGN DIRECT INVESTMENT AND CAPITAL FLIGHT

Library of Congress Cataloging-in-Publication Data

Kant, Chander.
Foreign direct investment and capital flight / Chander Kant.
p. cm. — (Princeton studies in international finance, ISSN 0081-8070 ; no. 80)
Includes bibliographical references.
ISBN 0-88165-252-0 (pbk.) : $11.00
1. Investments, Foreign—Developing countries. 2. Capital movements—Developing countries. 3. Saving and investment—Developing countries. I. Title. II. Series.
HG5993.K36 1996
332.6′73′091724—dc20 96-33923
CIP

Printed in the United States of America by Princeton University Printing Services at Princeton, New Jersey

International Standard Serial Number: 0081-8070

CONTENTS

TABLES

FIGURES

1 INTRODUCTION

Foreign direct investment (FDI) has been the largest single source of external finance for developing countries since 1993. Indeed, in 1995, the share of developing countries in global FDI inflows reached an historic high of 38 percent. Capital flight from the developing countries is also more extensive than was previously thought. For Latin America alone, residents are estimated to have about $300 billion in (potentially revertible) capital abroad (Kuczynski, 1992).[1] In addition, six of the ten countries having the highest average annual rates of capital flight from 1981 to 1991, and eight of the ten countries having the highest ratio of flight capital to external debt or to GDP, are countries outside Latin America (Claessens and Naudé, 1993).

Foreign debt and capital flight have been observed to accumulate simultaneously in the case of private external borrowing guaranteed by governments. It is natural to ask, therefore, if capital flight also occurs in conjunction with FDI inflows. Do FDI inflows facilitate capital flight, by increasing the availability of foreign exchange, or do they, instead, mark a reduction of capital flight or a gradual return of flight capital? Answers to these questions will shed light on the dominant causes of capital flight and foreign direct investment.

Because capital flight is a complex issue, most studies on the subject view it from one of two partial perspectives. One of these concentrates on the general investment climate affecting the attractiveness of source-country assets irrespective of who holds them. The other stresses the discriminatory treatment of residents' capital and differences between residents and nonresidents with regard to the actual or perceived risk in holding claims on residents. Similarly, foreign direct investment

I am grateful to an anonymous referee for detailed and helpful comments, to the World Bank Research Committee for financial support, and to Uma Ramakrishnan and Gail Morrison for support with data. The opinions expressed in this study do not necessarily represent those of the International Finance Corporation, the World Bank, or their boards of directors. An earlier version of this study was presented at the Allied Social Science Associations Meetings held in Washington, D.C., in January 1995. I would like to thank Guy Pfeffermann, Dale Weigel, Bob Miller, and Jack Glen for support and comments on the original version of the proposal.

[1] Here and throughout, "billion" means one thousand million.

might occur either because the general investment climate improves or because specific policies favor it.

Any analysis of the above two perspectives must confront differences in the definitions used for capital flight. Kindleberger (1937), for example, defines capital flight as "money that runs away," whereas Tornell and Velasco (1992) consider it to be all flows of productive resources from poor to rich countries. The exact amount of capital flight given by different definitions and measures also varies markedly. Because the robustness of any results can be established only if the same conclusions hold even with quite different measures of capital flight, this study addresses three questions.

- Do FDI inflows in developing countries facilitate capital flight (as private external borrowings do), or do they, instead, mark a reduction in capital flight or a return of flight capital?
- Does the relation between capital flight and foreign direct investment depend on the specific measure of capital flight used?
- Is the dominant cause of capital flight general economic mismanagement, or is it discriminatory treatment against residents' capital? Similarly, is foreign direct investment explained by a generally attractive investment climate, or is it explained by preferential treatment given specifically to such investment?

Chapter 2 presents the definition, measures, and sources of data for foreign direct investment for six developing-country regions from 1974 to 1992 and summarizes recent developments in FDI flows. Chapter 3 discusses various concepts of capital flight and the measures for which consistent sets of data have recently become available. The two alternative perspectives on the relation of capital flight to foreign direct investment are described in Chapter 4, and an empirical investigation of these connections is developed in Chapter 5. Chapter 6 summarizes the study's conclusions and presents their policy implications.

2 FOREIGN DIRECT INVESTMENT

The International Monetary Fund (IMF, 1993, section 359) defines foreign direct investment as an "investment that reflects the objective of obtaining a lasting interest by a resident entity in one economy in an enterprise resident in another economy. . . . The lasting interest implies the existence of a long-term relationship between the direct investor and the [foreign] enterprise and a significant degree of influence by the investor on the management of the enterprise." It is this sought-after element of influence and control that distinguishes direct from portfolio investment.

One statistical issue of interest is how to treat reinvested earnings from foreign direct investment. If capital flight is defined as all outflows from poor countries, irrespective of whether or not the outflow constitutes repatriated earnings of a nonresident, then reinvested earnings imply reduced capital flight. This is so because balance-of-payments accounting focuses on transactions involving an exchange of value between residents and nonresidents of a country, rather than an exchange of payments. Reinvestment of earnings from foreign direct investment is therefore treated as a capital inflow in the balance-of-payments statistics.

The IMF data on foreign direct investment are based on balance-of-payments reports from member countries and are host-country based. The other primary data on FDI are compiled by the Organisation for Economic Co-operation and Development (OECD), also for members, and are source-country based. Data from these two sources frequently differ. This is partly because many non-OECD countries are also sources of foreign direct investment. Foreign direct investment across developing countries, for example, is now rising rapidly, particularly in Asia; indeed, over 80 percent of the cumulative outward investment from developing countries in the past twenty years has taken place since 1985 (World Bank, 1993a). In order to include as many source countries of FDI as possible, I have used the IMF data in this study.

Some recent developments in foreign direct investment should be remarked. First, FDI in developing countries has only recently increased at high rates. From 1970 to 1980, it rose only slightly, from $3.7 billion to $4.7 billion, although commercial loans to oil importers during the same period trebled, and from 1981 to 1985, it actually declined, at an average annual rate of 4 percent. In 1986, however, the rate of investment began to increase, and from 1986 to 1990, it grew at an average annual rate of 17 percent. The increase since 1990 has been more dramatic. Although foreign direct investment has decreased globally since 1990, flows to developing countries have increased each year—by 40, 33, 47, 17, and 13 percent, respectively, for 1991 through 1995. The result is that developing countries now receive an unprecedented 38 percent of the world's total FDI. Second, the share of FDI in all external flows to developing countries is also high. Indeed, foreign direct investment is the main form of alternative financing found in the developing world—as opposed to traditional financing, which is guaranteed or intermediated by the public sector (Miller and Sumlinski, 1994; World Bank, 1995; UNCTAD, 1994).

Calvo, Leiderman, and Reinhart (1993) ask whether the recent massive capital inflows into Latin America will be followed by similar and sudden capital outflows, as occurred in the 1930s and mid-1980s, causing a domestic financial crisis. In contrast to the inflows during the 1920s, however, and during the years from 1978 to 1981, the largest single source of capital inflows to developing countries is now foreign direct investment. In 1991 and 1992, direct inflows for Latin America and the Caribbean constituted 33 percent of overall inflows (including both guaranteed and nonguaranteed loans as well as grants and technical assistance); portfolio inflows during those years accounted for only 18 percent of the total. The corresponding percentages for East Asia and the Pacific are 35 percent (FDI) and 6 percent (portfolio).

Claessens, Dooley, and Warner (1995) report that the time it takes for an unexpected shock to a flow to subside is about the same for both short- and long-term flows (as so labeled in the balance-of-payments data). Still, a direct investor is likely to take a longer view than a portfolio investor. A multinational corporation, for example, will probably have sunk costs, committed technology, and strategic objectives (a commitment to defend its brand name, for example). A direct inflow is thus likely to reverse more sluggishly as capital flight than a portfolio inflow will.

3 CAPITAL FLIGHT

One of the questions raised about foreign direct and portfolio inflows into developing countries is whether they mark the return of flight capital held abroad by the residents of those countries. There are varying estimates of the magnitude of residents' hoardings abroad. As mentioned above, Latin Americans are thought to have as much as $300 billion abroad (Kuczynski, 1992). According to the standard two-sector neoclassical growth model, the higher marginal product of capital in poor countries should induce capital to flow into rather than out of these countries.[2] The interest poor countries take in capital flight is precisely because it is counterintuitive.

Among the six regions of developing countries defined by the World Bank—East Asia and the Pacific, Europe and Central Asia, Latin America and the Caribbean, North Africa and the Middle East, South Asia, and Sub-Saharan Africa—Latin America accounts for the largest share of total capital flight, but capital flight is neither unique to Latin America nor more important to that region than to many other regions. Claessen and Naudé (1993) report, for example, that the ratio of flight-capital stock to GDP in 1991 was highest for North Africa and the Middle East (118 percent) and that the ratios for Sub-Saharan Africa (85 percent) and Europe and Central Asia (40 percent) were also higher than the ratios for Latin America and the Caribbean (35 percent). In East Asia and the Pacific, Korea and the Philippines have also experienced substantial capital flight. Capital flight is clearly important for virtually all regions of the developing world.

Any analysis of the relation of capital inflows to capital flight from developing countries must confront the differences in the definitions of capital flight. Kindleberger (1937, p. 158), who defines capital flight as "abnormal [flows] propelled from a country . . . by any one or more . . . fears and suspicions," emphasizes the volatile and abnormal nature of the outflows. Other economists include long-term capital flows in the definition of capital flight, on the grounds that many long-term flows

[2] The nonstandard model permits inefficiencies and imperfections in markets. Thus, Gertler and Rogoff (1990) show that (greater) capital-market inefficiencies in poorer countries may enable poor-country savers to enjoy higher returns abroad, even though under full information, they would do better to invest locally.

are also quite liquid. The broadest definition for capital flight is that used by Tornell and Velasco (1992), who define it as all flows of productive resources from poor to rich countries.

The exact amount of capital flight measured by the different definitions varies markedly. Eggerstedt, Hall, and Wijnbergen (1993), for example, report that using different definitions of capital flight changes the estimated amount of capital flight from Mexico for the 1970–85 period from a low of $26.5 billion to the high of $48.6 billion—that is, by a factor of almost two. In addition, no matter which method or source of data is used, there are usually large statistical errors involved in the calculations.

Most of the measures or definitions of capital flight are either direct or indirect.[3] The direct method of measurement identifies specific variables that constitute capital flight and seeks data directly for these variables. The indirect method defines capital flight indirectly, as, for example, a residual of some other variables. It also generally uses a broader definition of capital flight. These two methods of measurement and the different measures they use for capital flight are described below.

Direct Measures

The direct method seeks data from the balance-of-payments statistics. It identifies capital flight as one or more categories of short-term capital outflows and views it as a rapid response to investment risk.[4] It thus involves "hot money," money that responds quickly to political or financial crisis, to expectations of tighter capital controls or the devaluation of the domestic currency, or to changes in after-tax real returns. This is presumably also money that has the potential for returning quickly to the country when conditions change.

[3] Lessard and Williamson (1987) refer to these measures as the "balance-of-payments-accounts measure" and the "residual measure," terminology I avoid in this study, because the residual measure also relies substantially on balance-of-payments statistics.

[4] One group of direct measures identifies capital flight with trade misinvoicing and emphasizes the illegal nature of these outflows. Argentina, Mexico, and Venezuela had no exchange controls, however, when they experienced major episodes of capital flight. Furthermore, Gulati (1987) finds, in his study of nine major debtor countries (Argentina, Brazil, Chile, Korea, Mexico, Peru, the Philippines, Uruguay, and Venezuela) that underinvoicing of exports was outweighed by underinvoicing of imports, smuggling, or both (in an effort to mitigate the burden of *ad valorem* customs duties and quantitative restrictions).

A few direct measures of capital flight were recently proposed by Cuddington (1986, 1987). He defines capital flight as short-term "speculative" capital exports by the private nonbank sector, although in some cases banks and official entities may also be involved. Cuddington starts with the "errors and omissions" line in the balance-of-payments statistics. This line accounts for the difference between credit and debit entries in the balance of payments and is taken as a proxy variable for concealed or unrecorded short-term capital outflows (net of any concealed or unrecorded capital inflows). To this line is added data from the "other short-term capital, other sectors" line (that is, data that excludes the official sector and money-center banks). I call the total of these "Hot Money 2."

There are two variants of Hot Money 2. The first, which I call "Hot Money 1," adds only the "other assets" subcategory of the line item "other short-term capital, other sectors" to the "errors and omissions" line. This "other assets" subcategory means short-term capital flows that cannot fit into any other clearly defined category in the balance of payments. Hot Money 1 thus identifies capital flight with somewhat inexplicable flows across countries. The second variant, which I call "Hot Money 3," adds to Hot Money 2 the portfolio investments in bonds and corporate equity. Thus, to somewhat unknown flows, these volatile short-term capital movements are added. Note that in all three measures, numbers from the balance-of-payments data are multiplied by −1 so as to get positive numbers for capital flight.

There have been some criticisms of the direct method of measurement. The main ones are: (1) An investor, reacting to unfavorable conditions at home, is free to acquire different types of assets abroad: short-term, long-term, real (including real assets), and financial. The motivations for all such acquisitions, as well as their effects on the investor's home country, will generally be identical (although some assets, such as real estate, are considerably less liquid than others). (2) Even if one wishes to restrict oneself to components of those assets that can flow and reflow quickly, it seems best to look beyond short-term capital flows. Long-term foreign financial assets, for example, are close substitutes to short-term assets, because active and deep secondary markets in long-term assets exist. (3) The errors and omissions line includes not only unrecorded capital flows but also true measurement and rounding errors, unreported imports, and registration delays. In response to these criticisms, some authors have chosen to follow the indirect method of measuring capital flight.

Indirect Measures

In one version of the indirect method, capital flight is taken as a residual of four balance-of-payments components: the increase in debt owed to foreign residents, the net inflow of foreign direct investment, the increase in foreign-exchange reserves, and the amount of the current-account deficit. The premise is that the two inflows finance the two outflows, so that any inability of the two "sources of funds" to finance the two "uses of funds" is indicative of capital flight. Note that this view does not identify capital flight with a sudden response to policy changes. It attempts, instead, to measure the buildup of net foreign claims by the private sector without trying to distinguish between speculative or nonspeculative flows or between "normal" and "abnormal" flows.

One of the first such measures of capital flight was proposed in the World Bank's *World Development Report 1985* (WDR85). This measure differs from the Hot Money measures, not only in the method of measurement used, but also in the source of the data on foreign debt. Instead of using figures from the balance-of-payments statistics for the flow of foreign debt, the World Bank used its *World Debt Tables* to measure the year-to-year changes in the stock of foreign debt. There has been some criticism of this measure, because the stock of foreign debt may be affected by exchange-rate revaluations, debt reclassification and relief, and discoveries of existing debt. Claessens and Naudé (1993), however, have recently updated and corrected the WDR85 estimates by reducing the change in debt stock due to cross-country exchange-rate fluctuations, while adding back to the annual change the forgiven or reduced debt and debt service.

Two variations of the WDR85 measure are put forward by the Morgan Guaranty Trust (1986) and by Cline (1987). The Morgan Guaranty measure excludes from WDR85 the acquisition of short-term foreign assets by the country's banking system and monetary authorities. Thus, the accumulation of private foreign assets by the nonbanking sector only is identified as capital flight. Morgan Guaranty Trust (1986) offers no justification for treating the foreign acquisitions by firms and individuals differently from those by the banking system. One possible explanation is that the foreign-exchange transaction motive for holding these assets is likely to be far stronger for the banking than for the nonbanking sector.

The Cline method modifies the Morgan Guaranty measure by suggesting that reinvested investment income on bank deposits (and other assets) already held abroad should not be considered capital flight.

That is, if residents do not repatriate income from assets held abroad, this should not be considered as additional capital flight. Similarly, income from tourism and border transactions should be excluded from the current-account component of the residual measure, because these earnings are traded in the free rather than the official market.

The rationale for these adjustments is as follows. First, potential foreign creditors can only insist on reduction in the measure of capital flight as modified by Cline, because that amount is directly under the control of the debtor-country government. Second, it is the extent to which any inflow of funds is potentially available for additional capital flight that is significant. The presence of a surplus from tourism that is not garnered by the government or of private interest earnings abroad that are not repatriated has little to do with whether any freshly obtained capital is used as capital flight or otherwise.

The Dooley Measure

Dooley (1987) suggests using a hybrid measure of both direct and indirect methods of measurement. He defines capital flight as the stock of claims on nonresidents that do not generate investment-income receipts in the creditor country's balance-of-payments statistics. Although capital flight is defined directly by Dooley's method, there is no category or line in the balance-of-payments statistics that directly meets his definition. It is therefore necessary to compute indirectly the data for outflows motivated by a desire to place assets beyond the control of domestic authorities (to avoid the domestic risks associated with holding foreign earnings as domestic financial assets).

Dooley computes three measures of the total external position of the Philippines and of six Latin American countries (Argentina, Brazil, Chile, Mexico, Peru, and Venezuela) for the period from 1977 to 1984. These measures are the recorded external claims, the total external claims (both recorded and unrecorded), and the corrected total external claims. He then calculates the aggregate stock of recorded (private and official) claims on nonresidents—other than direct investment—from the cumulated balance-of-payments data. He estimates the initial value by capitalizing investment-income receipts during the first year and obtains total external (recorded and unrecorded) claims by adding unrecorded claims on nonresidents to the recorded claims. Dooley derives unrecorded claims by following a procedure similar to that used by Cuddington (1986), that is, the stock of errors and omissions in the cumulated balance-of-payments accounts is taken as a proxy measure for the unrecorded claims on nonresidents.

The balance-of-payments statistics, however, appear to underestimate the aggregate accumulation of cross-border claims. Dooley (1987) reports that, for the countries studied, nonresident claims on residents for 1984 were, as estimated from the balance-of-payments statistics, only about 60 percent as large as the amount of external debt estimated by the World Bank. Because a similar understatement is assumed for residents' claims on nonresidents, the total external claims (computed above) are scaled up by a corresponding factor. I call this scaled-up number the "corrected total external claims." This designation corresponds to what Dooley calls the "total *stock* of external claims" but is used here to avoid confusion with the second measure, "total external claims," which is also a stock.

The next step is to express investment-income receipts (as recorded on lines 15, 17, and 19 of the individual countries' detailed presentation tables of the IMF's *Balance of Payments Statistics Yearbook*, 1974–1992) as percentages of these three alternative measures of stocks of claims on nonresidents. The result is the calculated or implicit yields. Dooley (1987) observes that these calculated or implicit yields on total external claims and corrected total external claims are implausibly low in comparison to market yields, and he suggests that investment-income receipts as reported in the balance-of-payments data are systematically understated. To derive his numbers for capital flight, he therefore divides the receipts by market yields to obtain market-yield-equivalent capitalized values of actual investment-income receipts and then subtracts the result from "corrected total external claims" to get the measure for capital flight.

4 THE RELATION BETWEEN FOREIGN DIRECT INVESTMENT AND CAPITAL FLIGHT

During the debt crisis of the 1980s, it was feared that providing external funds to cash-starved developing countries would be futile if a large part of the increased lending were to flow right back out as capital flight. An erosion of debt inflows by capital flight during this period is, indeed, confirmed by both Cuddington (1987) and Pastor (1990). In the 1990s, however, the main sources of external finance to developing countries are nonguaranteed private inflows; the most important among these is foreign direct investment. Whether FDI inflows also facilitate capital flight or whether they inhibit it is a question generally examined from one of two perspectives. These are discussed below.

The Investment-Climate Perspective

From the investment-climate perspective, capital flight depends on the rate-of-return appeal of foreign as compared to domestic assets when adjusted for the exchange rate. The comparison is between returns attainable in the foreign country as opposed to those attainable at home; it is based on the location of the assets. Cuddington (1987) emphasizes this approach.

Cuddington employs a standard three-asset portfolio-adjustment model using domestic financial assets, domestic inflation hedges (such as land and buildings), and foreign financial assets. He defines capital flight as the year-to-year increase in domestic holdings of foreign financial assets. Amounts allocated to the different assets depend on the domestic interest rate, the foreign interest rate augmented by the rate of expected depreciation of the domestic currency, and the domestic inflation rate. In addition, he includes foreign lending to the country as a factor explaining capital flight.

Cuddington estimates his model using ordinary least-squares (OLS) regressions. He then reruns the regressions after deleting the insignificant variables and adding a lagged dependent variable on the right-hand side. For Mexico, Cuddington finds that foreign loan disbursements are a significant explanatory variable. In fact, the relevant coefficient value suggests that roughly $0.31 of each additional dollar of new long-term loans to Mexico from 1974 to 1984 flowed back out in the form of capital flight.

In another empirical study that finds a similar relation between foreign lending and capital flight, Pastor (1990) runs OLS regressions of capital flight (scaled by exports) from eight Latin American countries for 1973 to 1986. He uses the usual variables (the rate-of-return differential between U.S. and domestic financial assets and the domestic inflation rate) augmented by the degree of overvaluation of the exchange rate. Pastor (1990) analyzes the conclusions for robustness and searches for specification by adding one by one to the base regression the following structural (or real) variables: the ratio of net long-term borrowing to GDP (the capital-availability measure), the difference between the current year's and previous year's ratio of taxes to GDP, the difference between the country's growth rate and the lagged U.S. growth rate (as a proxy for relative profitability of investment in the domestic real sector—lagged because capital flight is itself thought to affect growth), and labor's share of GDP for the previous year (on the hypothesis that increase in this share dampens profitability and encourages capital flight). He finds that the ratio of net long-term borrowing to GDP is, at the 10 percent level, a statistically significant variable explaining capital flight.

The Discriminatory-Treatment Perspective

The discriminatory-treatment perspective does not relate capital flight to the usual determinants of net international capital movements, such as international-yield differentials. It highlights, instead, the fact that host countries often favor nonresident investment (and, by implication, discriminate against resident investment) in the form of differential taxation, investment or exchange-rate guarantees, and priority over resident claims in the event of a financial crisis. It is this discriminatory treatment, and the resulting differences in the actual or perceived risk by residents and nonresidents in holding claims on residents, that explains capital flight. This approach has been used by Khan and Ul Haque (1985), Eaton (1987), Dooley (1987) and Rojas-Suarez (1990), among others. Their models and analyses are briefly described below.

Khan and Ul Haque (1985) start with the standard intertemporal optimizing model of external borrowing and investment. At the beginning of the first period, households are endowed with a stock of domestic capital; this is used up during the first period and is transformed into output. The household may consume the first period's output; it may also invest that output, either at home or abroad. Investment abroad is risk free. Foreign borrowing is allowed, but it may be used only for domestic investment and may not be repudiated.

Domestic uncertainty is also permitted in the form of the possible expropriation of the domestic firm and its debt obligations with no compensation offered to the domestic owners of the expropriated assets, or, equivalently, domestic instability that reduces the firm to bankruptcy. Khan and Ul Haque (1985) show that positive values for both domestic and foreign investment are possible because of this uncertainty, even with positive levels of debt accumulation. Foreign lenders lend to the country because foreign debt may not be repudiated. At the same time, the risk of expropriation or of bankruptcy in the home country encourages capital flight.

Eaton (1987) builds on this work by first emphasizing that the risk of expropriation may also mean the threat of high levels of domestic taxation in the future. In addition, because foreign lenders generally have little ability to assess the solvency of a particular private borrower in a developing country, at least relative to the ability of the government of that country, loans for private borrowers may be channeled through the government, or lenders may require that such loans be guaranteed by the government of the borrower.

In contrast to Khan and Ul Haque, Eaton allows for the possibility that borrowers may invest borrowed funds abroad (foreign lenders may not, however, use these deposits as collateral against outstanding loans). The potential national takeover of private debt encourages a low level of effort by borrowers to service their debt and may even induce outright fraud. Because one borrower's default increases the expected value of the future tax obligations of other borrowers, the other borrowers' incentive to repay their debt diminishes and their incentive to place their funds abroad increases. Capital flight thus becomes contagious.

Dooley (1987) also uses the differences in the guarantees given by governments to foreign and domestic investment to explain the differences in the perceptions residents and nonresidents have regarding the risk-adjusted returns for claims held on residents. For nonresidents, the risk of default is the main concern. For residents, default is of less concern, because contracts between residents are better protected by the country's legal system than are contracts between residents and nonresidents. Fears of domestic inflation and exchange-rate depreciation, however, are of greater importance to residents than to nonresidents. Nonresident claims on debtor countries are typically denominated in foreign currencies, and although this fact alone does not make them immune to inflation and exchange-rate risk, they are less affected by these factors than are claims by residents.

Rojas-Suarez (1990) also refers to government guarantees to explain the simultaneous flight of capital from and large foreign loans to developing countries during the 1970s and early 1980s. She explains, in addition, that the debt crisis of the mid-1980s reduced, and perhaps eliminated, differences in risks faced by residents and nonresidents, so that domestic debt was no longer considered "junior."

The Hypotheses

As Lessard and Williamson (1987) point out, the investment-climate perspective cannot explain the simultaneous movement of capital into and out of the country.[5] By this explanation, capital flight depends on the attractiveness of foreign as compared to domestic assets—once the rate of return is adjusted for the exchange rate. Assets in the host country are either more or less attractive than assets in the foreign country, so that flows in both directions do not occur. The discriminatory-treatment perspective, however, can explain simultaneous flows. In fact, this explanation was specifically put forward to explain the coexistence of private foreign lending (implicitly or explicitly guaranteed by governments) and capital flight.

As remarked above, the major capital inflow to developing countries in recent years has been, not international lending, but private foreign investment, in which the foreign investor faces the additional risk of variability in the nominal value of his return. The factors affecting international lending, however, are also applicable to private foreign investment. Both foreign lenders and investors find it difficult to assess the solvency (or profitability) of a particular private borrower (or project) in a developing country, and both are subject to a far greater risk of market failure resulting from the relative nonenforceability of contracts for foreign as compared with domestic lending or investment. Private foreign investors (as well as foreign lenders) may therefore require that their investments be guaranteed or at least be favorably treated by the recipient's government. Many developing-country governments do, as mentioned, offer private investors favorable treatment in the form of differential taxation, investment or exchange-rate guarantees, or priority over resident claims in the event of financial crisis.

[5] Generally, rather than borrowing themselves from the private external market, governments give implicit or explicit guarantees to borrowings by private entities. As discussed above, Eaton (1987) argues that by guaranteeing external, but not internal, borrowing, governments encourage roundtrip flows in the form of capital flight.

The investment-climate perspective suggests that capital flight ought to decrease if the investment climate improves and foreign direct investment increases; the relation between FDI inflows and capital flight will therefore be negative. If, however, foreign direct investment is the result of preferential treatment given to foreign as compared with domestic investment, FDI inflows will likely be accompanied by continued and accelerated capital flight; the relation between the two will therefore be positive.

If the discriminatory-treatment view overrides the investment-climate perspective and FDI inflows occur, a capital inflow of one kind will be accompanied by an outflow of another kind, so that the net effect of the inflow will be minimal. In this event, specific policies such as tax amnesties or treaties, the offering of domestic instruments denominated in foreign currencies, and capital-control programs may be needed to restrain outflows of capital and to induce repatriation of flight capital. If the investment-climate explanation is dominant, however, and the relation between capital flight and FDI inflows is negative, the policies that stimulate investment in general will also entice flight capital to return and capital flight to decrease, so that the effect of FDI inflows on the economy will be magnified. Although this question has important policy implications, it has not been studied in the literature.

Numerous studies have analyzed the relation of foreign direct investment to real variables such as technology transfers and exports, but there have been virtually no inquiries into the financial or monetary effects of foreign direct investment (Kant, 1990, discusses only its fiscal or budgetary effects). Because many developing countries are only now emerging from the debt crisis (partly caused by capital flight) following the 1978–81 boom in commercial bank loans, their wariness regarding the short- and long-term financial implications of the current spurt in private FDI (as well as portfolio) investment is not surprising. This study attempts to determine whether such inflows themselves facilitate capital flight or whether they reduce it.

5 AN EMPIRICAL EXAMINATION OF THE RELATION BETWEEN FOREIGN DIRECT INVESTMENT AND CAPITAL FLIGHT

One problem in using the residual measure for examining the relation of capital flight to foreign direct investment is that foreign direct investment is also a component of the residual measure. Although the other three components (the increase in foreign indebtedness, the increase in reserves, and the amount of the current-account deficit, may overwhelm foreign direct investment, its mere presence as a positive component gives a positive bias to any connection between FDI and the residual measure of capital flight. Finding a negative connection between foreign direct investment and the residual measure will therefore be a particularly strong result.

The following analysis uses one specific variant of the residual measure. To check the reliability of the relationship revealed by using a residual measure and to present a comprehensive analysis (because there is no consensus on a single definition or measure for capital flight), the hypothesized connections are also examined by using one direct measure and the sole hybrid (Dooley) measure. The criteria used to select one from among the different variants of direct and residual measures are consistency and the strength of the relationship revealed; the measure that reveals the most consistent (whether consistently positive or consistently negative) relationship in either category is selected. On this basis, Hot Money 3 is selected from the direct measures, and Cline is selected from the residual measures. Note that these measures take a somewhat broad view of capital flight.[6]

Data and Estimation

The two main sources of data are the World Bank and the IMF. The World Bank has recently computed estimates of capital flight for each

[6] Admittedly, a significant portion of capital outflows from developing countries consists of outward FDI, especially since 1985 (China, a low-income country, is the most important developing-country exporter of FDI). Because only net FDI inflow (net of outflow) is taken as a source of funds, these outflows are not included in the Cline or Dooley measures. The direct measure, Hot Money 3, excludes outward FDI flows from its definition of capital flight.

of the above three measures for all developing countries from 1974 to 1992 (I include as "developing" all those countries defined by the World Bank as "low-" or "middle-income"). Similar estimates have also been calculated for all the countries in the six geographical regions. These are the capital-flight data used in this study. Group or regional data are used, rather than country data, because they are less apt to be affected by random factors.

Data on foreign direct investment have been taken from the IMF's balance-of-payments statistics. Because the IMF defines developing countries differently than the World Bank and does not provide data for comparable geographical groupings, I have grouped the IMF country data to agree with the World Bank's geographical regions and have added together the regional totals to yield the FDI inflows for all developing countries.[7]

Portfolio (that is, other than direct) investment is the other private inflow. Gooptu (1993) estimates portfolio inflows for many developing countries by incorporating information from sources that include securities firms, major banks, European publications, the IMF, and the World Bank. His data are compiled only from 1989, however, and are not available for some developing countries. To achieve more comprehensive coverage and to ensure consistency in distinguishing between portfolio and direct investment, I have therefore used the IMF's balance-of-payments data for portfolio inflows as well as for direct flows (although it should be recognized that all portfolio inflows may not be recorded in these data). The totals of portfolio inflows are calculated for each of the six regions and the developing countries as a group in the same manner as for foreign direct investment.

My estimation method is by contemporaneous-correlation and principal-component analysis, rather than regression analysis, because I have no basis for hypothesizing that either capital flight or the private inflow (FDI or portfolio) is the independent (or dependent) variable. Although I have stated above that the sign of co-movement conveys information about the reason for FDI inflows and capital flight, much additional analysis is needed to determine causality and the exact

[7] The World Bank defines as "developing" all countries with a 1991 GNP per capita income of less than $7,911. The IMF follows the UN definition of developed areas and designates all countries other than Australia, Canada, Japan, New Zealand, South Africa, Turkey, the United States, and those in Western Europe as "developing." For a list of countries not called "developing" by the World Bank, see *World Development Report 1993* (1993), pp. 326–327.

transmission of the relation between these variables. Simple measures of association nevertheless provide a useful start. These associations are examined in turn for direct and portfolio inflows for each of the three measures of capital flight discussed above, for all six of the regions, and for all the developing countries.

Results

The results from contemporaneous-correlation and principal-component analysis are presented in turn. Note, first, that the balance-of-payments statistics provide no data on portfolio flows to Sub-Saharan Africa or to North Africa and the Middle East for the 1974–92 period. For these two regions, it is clearly not possible to test for the relation between portfolio flows and capital flight. Data on FDI flows for these regions are available, as are data on both kinds of private flows to South Asia, but in none of the three areas, are FDI (or in South Asia, portfolio) flows significantly related to any of the three measures of capital flight. No definite conclusions can be reached, therefore, by analyzing the data for these regions.[8] Data on foreign direct and portfolio inflows for the remaining three regions and for all developing countries as a group are shown in Tables 1 and 2. Capital-flight data for all developing countries are presented in Table 3. Figures 1, 2 and 3 show data for East Asia and the Pacific, Europe and the Mediterranean, and Latin America and the Caribbean.

Table 4 presents statistically significant results from contemporaneous-correlation analysis for the developing countries as a group, as well as for East Asia and the Pacific, Europe and the Mediterranean, and Latin America and the Caribbean. The first number for each measure of capital flight gives the estimated sample correlation coefficient. The number in parentheses gives the cumulated probability that the population correlation coefficient will be greater than the absolute value of the sample correlation coefficient under the null hypothesis that the population correlation coefficient is zero. The 5 percent level of significance is used to select the correlations presented.

Three sets of conclusions can be drawn from Table 4. Note that the results are based on time-series data for 1974 to 1992 and that the data cover regions as divergent in economic policies and experiences as East Asia and Latin America. The first observation is that foreign direct

[8] Similarly, none of the other variants of direct and residual measures of capital flight described above is significantly related to either category of private flows to these three regions. Detailed results are available from the author.

TABLE 1

FDI INFLOWS FOR COUNTRY GROUPS
(in millions of U.S. dollars)

Year	East Asia and the Pacific	Latin America and the Caribbean	Europe and the Mediterranean	All Developing Countries
1974	847	1,772	247	581
1975	1,025	3,265	269	7,375
1976	1,042	1,761	398	3,544
1977	1,076	3,163	495	6,297
1978	1,068	4,095	574	7,165
1979	954	5,482	812	7,775
1980	1,318	6,182	883	5,178
1981	2,084	8,011	846	19,323
1982	2,458	6,190	669	22,455
1983	2,888	3,518	671	13,687
1984	2,946	3,237	846	14,149
1985	3,183	4,090	854	11,356
1986	3,546	3,672	872	11,096
1987	4,485	5,790	1,295	12,961
1988	7,595	7,955	2,238	20,655
1989	9,074	7,049	3,471	23,730
1990	10,683	7,595	4,644	27,222
1991	13,585	12,306	6,842	35,728
1992	20,387	14,349	7,240	45,208

SOURCE: Data compiled from IMF, *Balance of Payments Statistics Tape*, June 1994.

investment is invariably negatively related to capital flight. In contrast to external borrowings guaranteed by governments, FDI inflows may therefore be expected to reduce capital flight and to have magnified effects on the economy. In fact, for every $1 increase in FDI inflows, capital flight may be expected to decrease by $0.50 to $0.84. Second, a similar relationship holds for portfolio inflows and capital flight.[9] Third, the dominant reason for FDI inflows (and reduced capital flight) is not specific policies favoring foreign (and discriminating against domestic) investment; it is, instead, an improvement in the general investment climate.

[9] Even for the other three regions, where the coefficients are not statistically significant for any of the measures discussed, the sign is negative for thirteen of a total of eighteen contemporaneous-correlation coefficients computed.

TABLE 2

PORTFOLIO EQUITY INFLOWS FOR COUNTRY GROUPS
(in millions of U.S. dollars)

Year	East Asia and the Pacific	Latin America and the Caribbean	Europe and the Mediterranean	All Developing Countries
1974	NA	NA	NA	NA
1975	NA	NA	NA	NA
1976	NA	NA	NA	NA
1977	NA	NA	NA	NA
1978	NA	NA	NA	NA
1979	NA	NA	NA	NA
1980	NA	NA	NA	NA
1981	53	135	NA	188
1982	NA	NA	NA	NA
1983	NA	NA	NA	NA
1984	150	NA	NA	150
1985	138	NA	NA	138
1986	31	NA	192	383
1987	405	78	NA	483
1988	730	176	56	1,073
1989	2,623	434	168	3,344
1990	2,268	1,099	105	3,608
1991	1,039	6,228	23	7,312
1992	4,477	7,883	252	12,869

SOURCE: Data compiled from IMF, *Balance of Payments Statistics Tape*, June 1994.

All three methods of measuring capital flight give similar values of contemporaneous-correlation coefficients and probability values. Thus, despite the torturously indirect route used by the Dooley method, and contrary to Gordon's and Levine's (1989) conclusion that statistical problems make it unreliable, the Dooley measure still gives consistently negative results for the three regions and for the developing countries as a group. In fact, of all the measures analyzed, it has the strongest (negative) association with portfolio inflows—except with respect to Latin America and the Caribbean, for which the Cline measure is marginally stronger. No such clear dominance emerges for the relationship of capital flight to FDI inflows. For the developing countries as a group, however, both the Cline and Hot Money 3 measures have equally strong, negative relationships. Figures 4, 5, and 6 chart the three capital-flight measures for all developing countries against the total FDI numbers.

TABLE 3

CAPITAL FLIGHT FROM ALL DEVELOPING COUNTRIES
(*in millions of U.S. dollars*)

Year	Cline	Dooley	Hot Money 3
1974	-8,390.3	-15,211.8	5,038.4
1975	-4,805.9	-12,010.7	4,824.9
1976	-15,773.7	-6,954.1	11,339.8
1977	41,494.1	52,229.4	3,613.2
1978	-12,514.5	9,764.5	5,447.9
1979	-3,133.0	19,816.4	3,551.7
1980	4,709.8	-2,457.3	5,230.0
1981	-20,625.5	25,793.4	18,038.0
1982	-162.1	40,051.0	26,665.5
1983	7,182.5	61,200.0	21,088.4
1984	-5,059.5	33,108.4	16,236.9
1985	566.8	15,125.3	9,044.4
1986	31,914.0	56,219.5	-6,720.0
1987	64,597.3	122,104.0	445.9
1988	69,826.8	148,051.0	1,328.4
1989	-75,143.6	-8,081.5	-2,248.1
1990	-73,730.1	-81,033.8	-13,435.2
1991	-66,954.8	-112,591.5	-30,273.7
1992	-154,379.8	-377,157.7	-44,818.7

SOURCE: World Bank, *Capital Flight Estimates*, October 1994.

Swoboda (1983) and Calvo, Leiderman, and Reinhart (1993) suggest that principal-components analysis is convenient for determining whether a common element (or a number of common elements) can explain the variance of a number of individual time series. Principal components are linear combinations of the original variables that explain increasingly higher proportions of the total variance of those variables. A set of series for which the variances have a strong common element will require fewer principal components to explain a large fraction of the total variance (Dhrymes, 1974).

Table 5 reports the cumulative percentage of variance (CPV) explained and the factor loadings on the first principal component for foreign direct investment and for each of the three measures of capital flight. The factor loadings are measures of the association of each series with the first principal component. The factor loading of a variable is, in fact, the regression coefficient of the variable on the appropriate principal component.

FIGURE 1

Capital Flight from East Asia and the Pacific

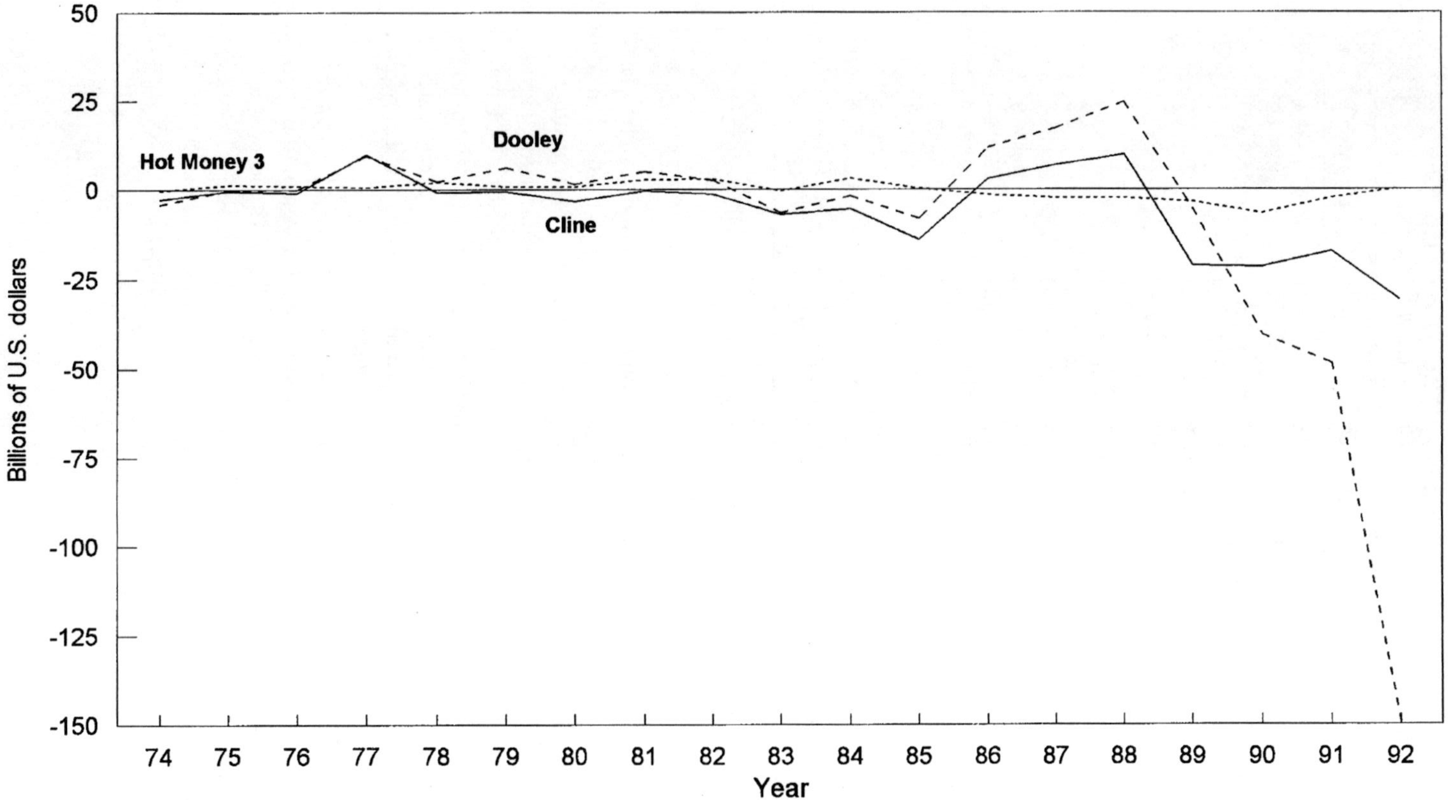

FIGURE 2

CAPITAL FLIGHT FROM EUROPE AND THE MEDITERRANEAN

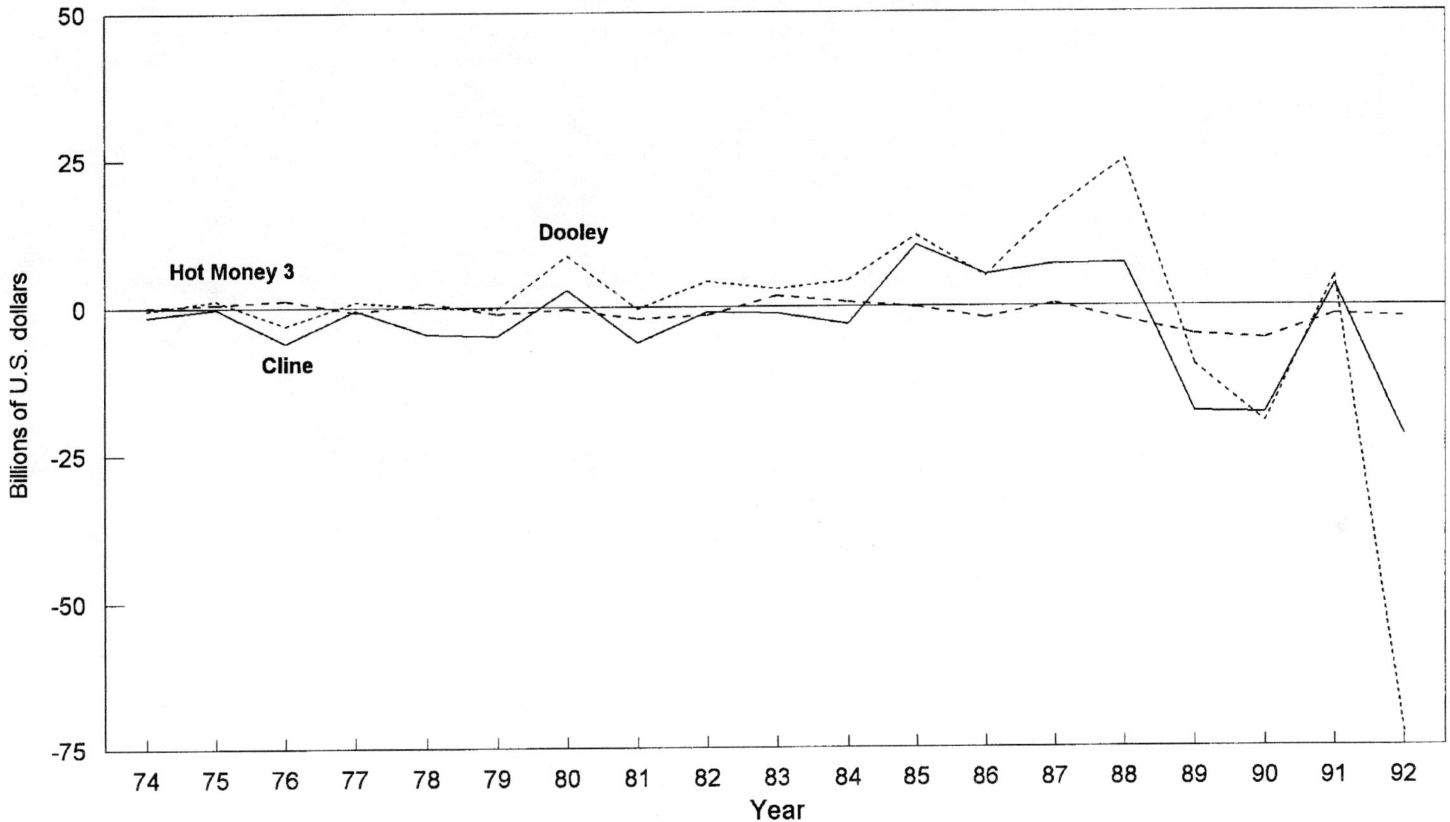

FIGURE 3

CAPITAL FLIGHT FROM LATIN AMERICA AND THE CARIBBEAN

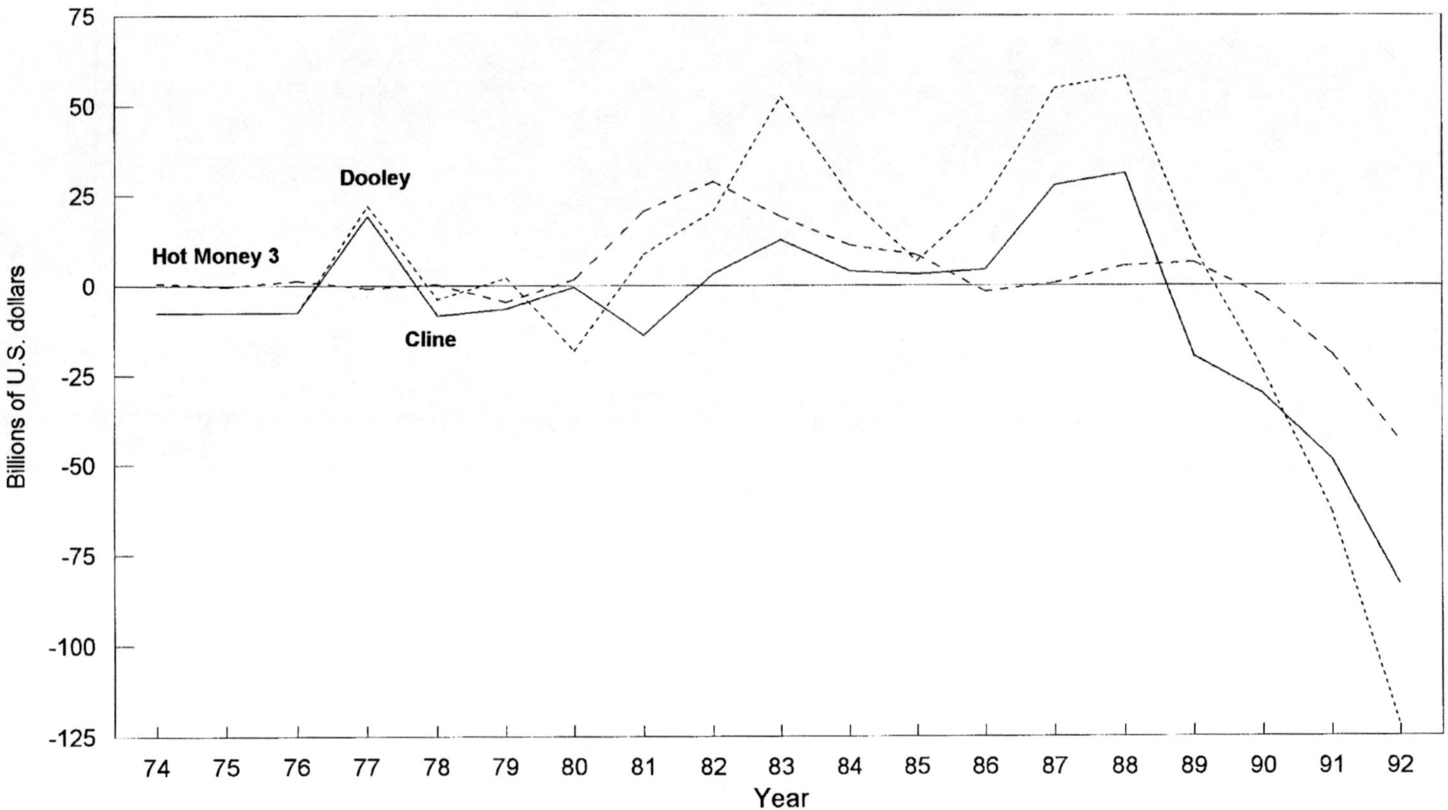

FIGURE 4

The Cline Measure and FDI: All Developing Countries

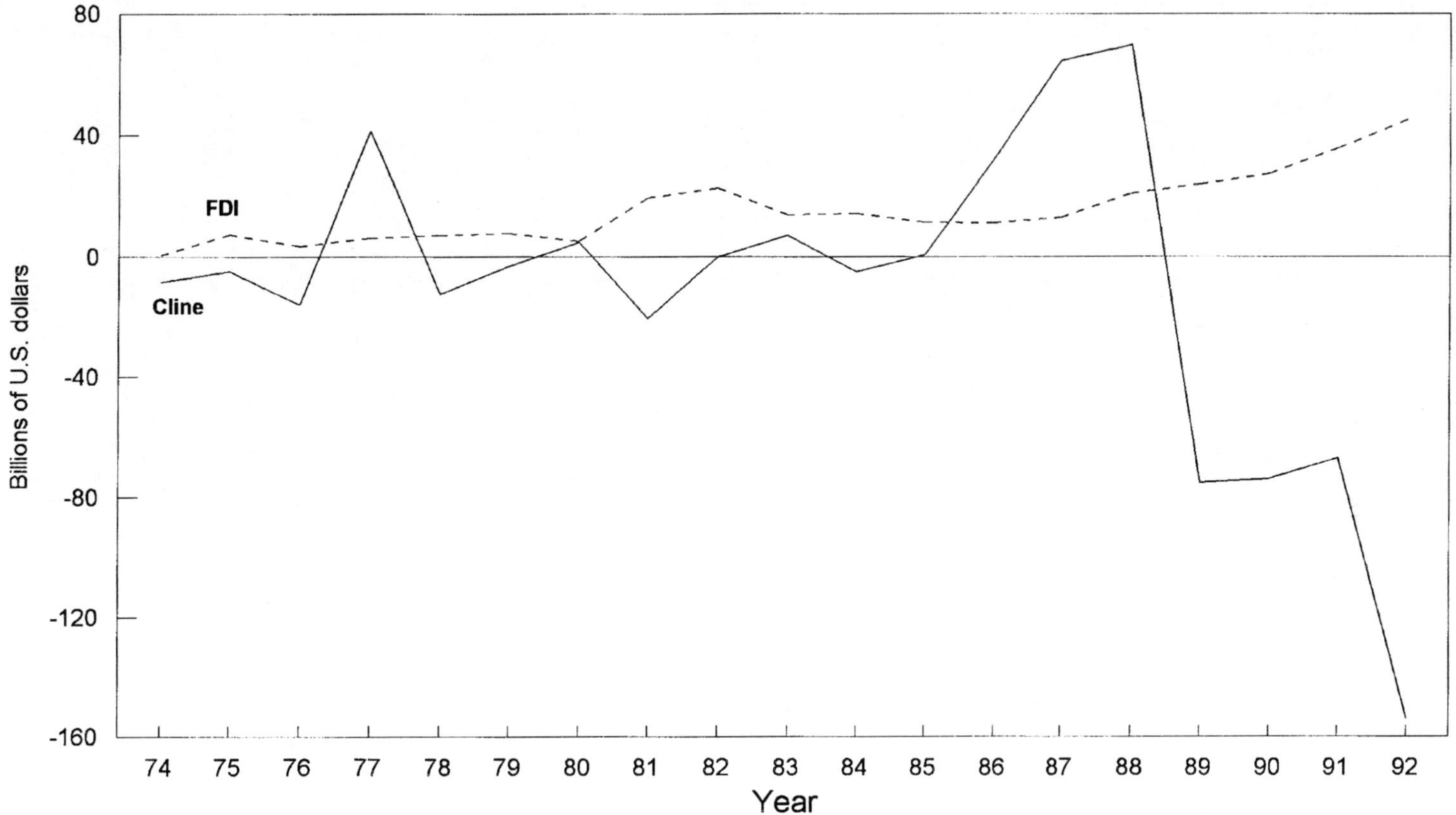

FIGURE 5

THE DOOLEY MEASURE AND FDI: ALL DEVELOPING COUNTRIES

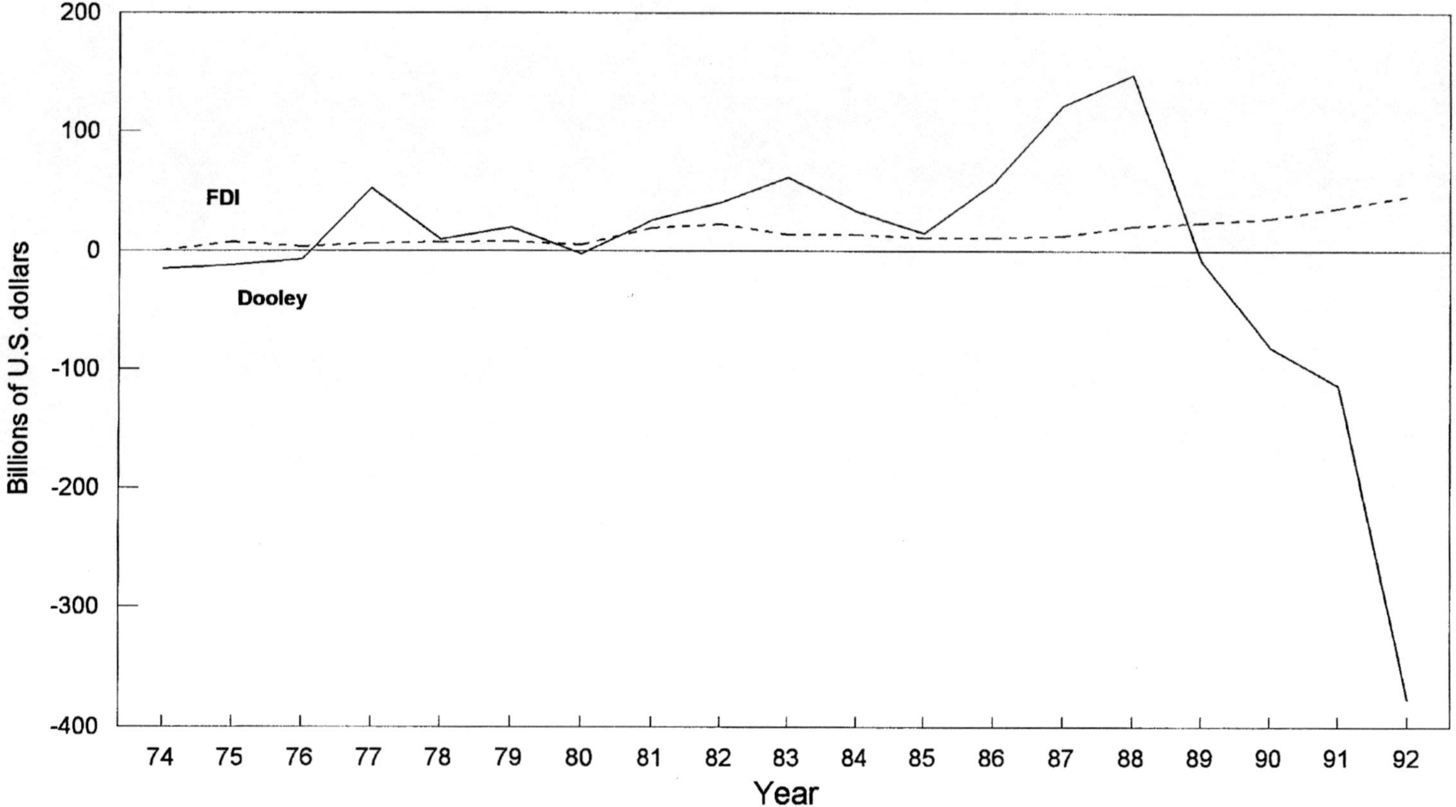

FIGURE 6

THE HOT MONEY 3 MEASURE AND FDI: ALL DEVELOPING COUNTRIES

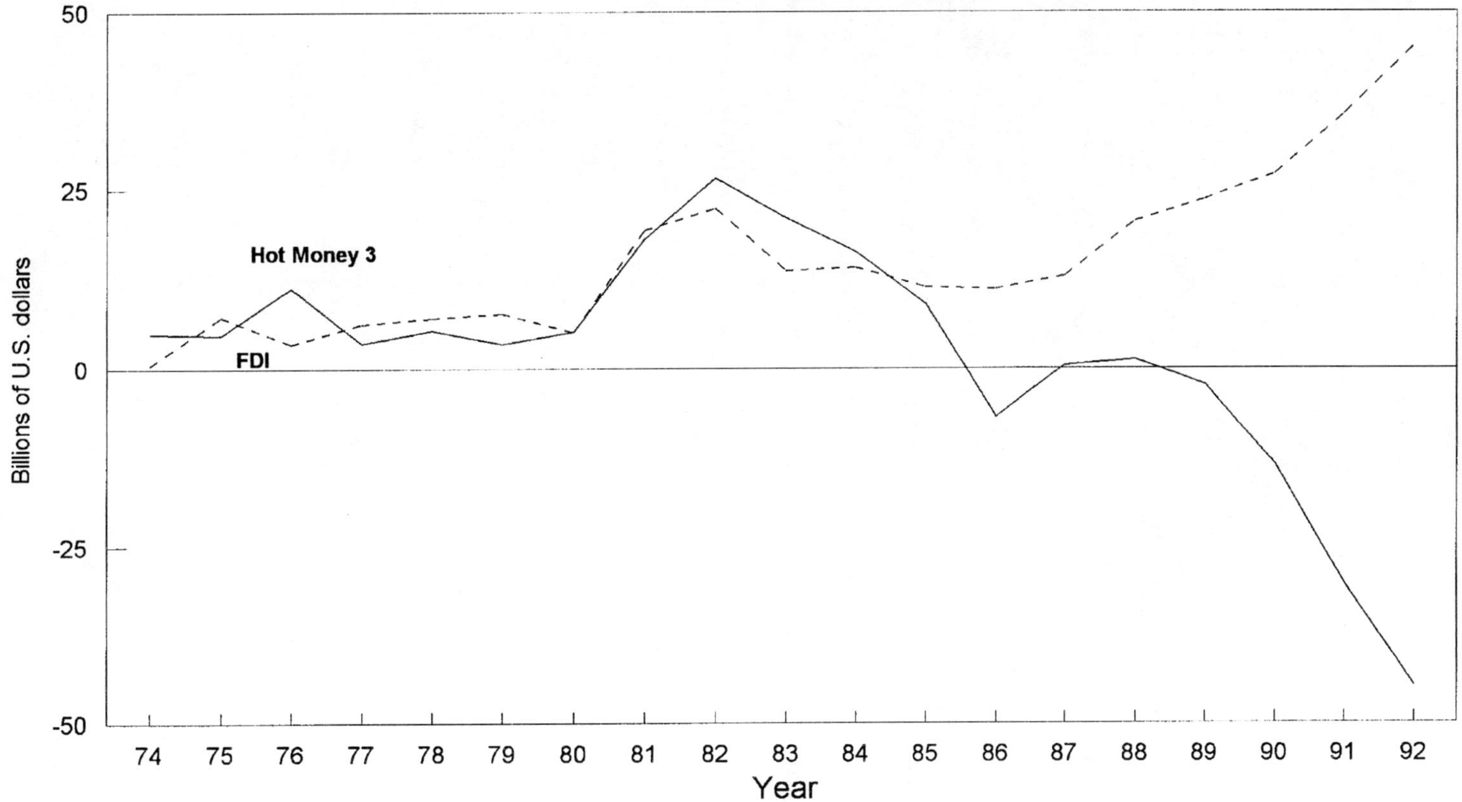

TABLE 4

CORRELATIONS BETWEEN DIFFERENT CAPITAL-FLIGHT MEASURES AND FDI AND PORTFOLIO FLOWS, 1974–1992

Capital-Flight Measures	East Asia and the Pacific		Europe and the Mediterranean		Latin America and the Caribbean		All Developing Countries	
	FDI	Portfolio	FDI	Portfolio	FDI	Portfolio	FDI	Portfolio
Cline	−0.76 (0.00)	−0.80 (0.00)	−0.50 (0.03)	−0.56 (0.01)	−0.72 (0.00)	−0.85 (0.00)	−0.71 (0.00)	−0.81 (0.00)
Dooley	−0.84 (0.00)	−0.83 (0.00)	−0.62 (0.00)	−0.68 (0.00)	−0.65 (0.00)	−0.84 (0.00)	−0.66 (0.00)	−0.88 (0.00)
Hot Money 3	−0.50 (0.03)	−0.47 (0.04)	−0.57 (0.01)	−0.61 (0.00)	−0.57 (0.01)	−0.80 (0.00)	−0.71 (0.00)	−0.87 (0.00)

NOTE: Numbers in parentheses indicate the significance level.

The findings of correlation analysis are confirmed by the results of the principal-component analysis. The factor loadings for capital flight are uniformly negative, and those for direct and portfolio inflows are uniformly positive. As expected, factor loadings are found to be consistently high for the three measures selected; this supports the conclusions found earlier.

TABLE 5

FIRST PRINCIPAL COMPONENTS FOR DIFFERENT CAPITAL-FLIGHT MEASURES: FACTOR LOADINGS AND THE CUMULATIVE PERCENTAGE OF VARIANCE (CPV) EXPLAINED BY THE FIRST PRINCIPAL COMPONENT

Capital-Flight Measures	East Asia and the Pacific				Europe and the Mediterranean				Latin America and the Caribbean				All Developing Countries			
	Capital Flight	FDI	Portfolio	CPV	Capital Flight	FDI	Portfolio	CPV	Capital Flight	FDI	Portfolio	CPV	Capital Flight	FDI	Portfolio	CPV
Cline	−0.56	0.58	0.59	88	−0.55	0.58	0.60	71	−0.57	0.57	0.60	87	−0.46	0.62	0.64	73
Dooley	−0.57	0.58	0.58	91	−0.58	0.57	0.58	76	−0.56	0.56	0.60	85	−0.53	0.58	0.62	81
Hot Money 3	−0.47	0.63	0.62	76	−0.57	0.57	0.59	74	−0.55	0.56	0.61	83	−0.52	0.61	0.59	80

NOTE: Principal components are linear combinations of the original variables that explain increasingly higher proportions of the total variance of those variables are measures of the association of each series (Capital Flight, FDI, and Portfolio) with the first principal component.

6 SUMMARY AND CONCLUSIONS

Despite the increasing importance of foreign direct investment for developing countries, little attention has been given to its financial effects in general or its relation to capital flight in particular.

It has been found that 31 to 40 percent of the private external borrowing guaranteed by developing-country governments leaves as capital flight. The first question explored in this study has been whether FDI inflows similarly facilitate capital flight from developing countries.

A second question has been whether it is the investment climate or the discriminatory treatment favoring nonresident investment that is the determining cause of capital flight. This question is examined through direct, indirect, and hybrid measures.

There is no consensus on a single definition of capital flight, and the exact amount of capital flight given by different measures and definitions varies markedly. The direct method of measurement seeks data for those specific variables identified as constituting capital flight. This method associates capital flight with one or more categories of short-term capital outflows and views it as a rapid response to investment risk. The indirect method regards capital flight as a residual of four balance-of-payments components: the increase in debt owed to foreign residents, the net inflow of foreign direct investment, the increase in foreign-exchange reserves, and the amount of the current-account deficit. It implies that the two inflows finance the two outflows, so that any inability of the two "sources of funds" to finance the two "uses of funds" is indicative of capital flight. The Dooley method defines capital flight directly—that is, as the stock of claims on nonresidents that do not generate investment-income receipts in the creditor country's balance of payments—but must compute data for these outflows very indirectly.

Hot Money 3, the direct measure used in this study, is obtained by adding, from the IMF's balance-of-payments statistics, the lines for "errors and omissions," "other short-term capital," and "other sectors" (but excluding the "official" sector and "money-center banks") to the portfolio investments in both bonds and corporate equity. The Cline measure, an indirect measure, excludes from the basic residual measure the acquisition of short-term foreign assets by the banking system and monetary authorities, reinvested investment income earned on bank deposits (and other assets) already held abroad, and income from tourism and other border transactions. The Dooley measure, although defining capital flight directly, must compute data for the outflows very indirectly, as described above in Chapter 3.

I use World Bank (1994) estimates for the capital-flight measures and compute from the IMF's balance-of-payments figures data for foreign direct and portfolio investment that conform to the World Bank's geographical groupings. The estimation methods used are contemporaneous-correlation and principal-component analysis.

My first finding is that FDI inflows are always associated with a reduction in capital flight. This conclusion holds for all three capital-flight measures used, even though these measures are computed in very different ways and yield quite different numbers. The second conclusion is that capital flight is primarily caused by general economic mismanagement and inefficiencies rather than by preferential treatment of foreign capital. This finding is quite consistent with the Gertler-Rogoff (1990) model cited above. Policies that reduce capital-market frictions will both encourage capital inflows and discourage capital flight.

The first result implies that FDI inflows can be expected to have magnified effects on the host economy. Indeed, because broad definitions are used for capital flight, the effect of these inflows will be even greater. The second finding suggests that this magnified effect can be obtained by improving the macroeconomic management of the economy.

These conclusions are particularly significant for policy development in developing countries. A large number of these countries are now seeking FDI inflows. They also want to stem capital flight or to induce flight capital to return. The results of these analyses suggest that their efforts are likely to be more successful if they improve the overall investment climate in their economies than if they give favored treatment to nonresident investment.

REFERENCES

Calvo, Guillermo A., Leonardo Leiderman, and Carmen M. Reinhart, "Capital Inflows and Real Exchange Rate Appreciation in Latin America," *International Monetary Fund Staff Papers*, 40 (1993), pp. 108–151.

Claessens, Stijn, Michael P. Dooley, and Andrew Warner, "Portfolio Capital Flows: Hot or Cold," *World Bank Economic Review*, 9 (1995), pp. 153–174

Claessens, Stijn, and David Naudé, "Recent Estimates of Capital Flight," World Bank Policy Research Working Paper No. 1186, Washington, D.C., World Bank, 1993.

Cline, William R., "Discussion" (of Chapter 3), in Donald R. Lessard and John Williamson, eds., *Capital Flight and Third World Debt*, Washington, D.C., Institute for International Economics, 1987.

Cuddington, John T., *Capital Flight: Estimates, Issues, and Explanations*, Princeton Studies in International Finance No. 58, Princeton, N.J., Princeton University, International Finance Section, December 1986.

———, "Capital Flight," *European Economic Review*, 31 (1987), pp. 382–388.

Dhrymes, Phoebus J., *Econometrics: Statistical Foundations and Applications*, New York, Springer-Verlag, 1974.

Dooley, Michael P., "Capital Flight, A Response to Differences in Financial Risks," *International Monetary Fund Staff Papers*, 34 (1987), pp. 422–436.

Eaton, Jonathan, "Public Debt Guarantees and Private Capital Flight," *World Bank Economic Review*, 1 (1987), pp. 377–395.

Eggerstedt, Herald, Rebecca B. Hall, and Sweder van Wijnbergen, "Measuring Capital Flight, A Case Study of Mexico," World Bank Policy Research Working Paper No. 1121, Washington, D.C., World Bank, 1993.

Gertler, Mark, and Kenneth Rogoff, "North-South Lending and Endogenous Domestic Capital Market Inefficiencies," *Journal of Monetary Economics*, 26 (1990), pp. 245–266.

Gooptu, Sudarshan, "Portfolio Investment Flows to Emerging Markets," in Stijn Claessens and Sudarshan Gooptu, eds., *Portfolio Investment in Developing Countries*, World Bank Discussion Paper No. 228, Washington, D.C., World Bank, 1993.

Gordon, David R., and Ross Levine, "The Problem of Capital Flight: A Cautionary Note," *World Economy*, 12 (1989), pp. 237–252.

Gulati, Sunil, "A Note on Trade Misinvoicing," in Donald R. Lessard and John Williamson, eds., *Capital Flight and Third World Debt*, Washington, D.C., Institute for International Economics, 1987.

International Monetary Fund (IMF), *Balance of Payments Manual*, 5th ed., Washington, D.C., International Monetary Fund, 1993.

———, *Balance of Payments Statistics Tape* (computer tape), Washington, D.C., International Monetary Fund, June 1994

———, *Balance of Payments Statistics Yearbook*, Part 1, Washington, D.C., International Monetary Fund, 1974–1992.

Kant, Chander, "Multinational Firms and Government Revenues," *Journal of Public Economics*, 42 (1990), pp. 135–147.

Khan, Moshin S., and Nadeem Ul Haque, "Foreign Borrowing and Capital Flight," *International Monetary Fund Staff Papers*, 32 (1985), pp. 2–15.

Kindleberger, Charles P., *International Short-Term Capital Movements*, New York, Augustus Kelley, 1937.

Kuczynski, Pedro-Pablo, "International Capital Flows into Latin America: What is the Promise?" in Lawrence H. Summers and Anwar M. Shah, eds., *Proceedings of the World Bank Annual Conference on Development Economics*, Washington, D.C., World Bank, 1992.

Lessard, Donald R., and John Williamson, eds., *Capital Flight and Third World Debt*, Washington, D.C., Institute for International Economics, 1987.

Miller, Robert R., and Mariusz A. Sumlinski, "Trends in Private Investment in Developing Countries 1994," International Finance Corporation Discussion Paper No. 20, Washington, D.C., World Bank, 1994.

Morgan Guaranty Trust Company, "LDC Capital Flight," *World Financial Markets*, March (1986), pp. 13–15.

Pastor, Manuel, Jr., "Capital Flight from Latin America", *World Development*, 18 (1990), pp. 1–18.

Rojas-Suarez, Liliana, "Risk and Capital Flight in Developing Countries," International Monetary Fund Working Paper No. 90/64, Washington, D.C., International Monetary Fund, 1990.

Swoboda, Alexander K., "Exchange Rate Regimes and U.S.-European Policy Interdependence," *International Monetary Fund Staff Papers*, 30 (1983), pp. 75–102.

Tornell, Aaron, and Andrés Velasco, "The Tragedy of the Commons and Economic Growth: Why Does Capital Flow from Poor to Rich Countries?" *Journal of Political Economy*, 100 (1992), pp. 1208–1231.

United Nations Conference on Trade and Development (UNCTAD), *World Investment Report, 1994: Transnational Corporations, Employment and the Work Place*, Division of Transnational Corporations and Investment, New York, UNCTAD, 1994.

World Bank, *Capital Flight Estimates* (computer diskette), International Economics Department, Washington, D.C., World Bank, October 1944.

———, World Debt Tables, Vols. 1, 1993–1994 and 1995–1996, Washington, D.C., World Bank, 1993a; 1995.

———, *World Development Report 1985* and . . . *1994*, Washington, D.C., World Bank, 1985; 1993b.

PUBLICATIONS OF THE INTERNATIONAL FINANCE SECTION

Notice to Contributors

The International Finance Section publishes papers in four series: ESSAYS IN INTERNATIONAL FINANCE, PRINCETON STUDIES IN INTERNATIONAL FINANCE, and SPECIAL PAPERS IN INTERNATIONAL ECONOMICS contain new work not published elsewhere. REPRINTS IN INTERNATIONAL FINANCE reproduce journal articles previously published by Princeton faculty members associated with the Section. The Section welcomes the submission of manuscripts for publication under the following guidelines:

ESSAYS are meant to disseminate new views about international financial matters and should be accessible to well-informed nonspecialists as well as to professional economists. Technical terms, tables, and charts should be used sparingly; mathematics should be avoided.

STUDIES are devoted to new research on international finance, with preference given to empirical work. They should be comparable in originality and technical proficiency to papers published in leading economic journals. They should be of medium length, longer than a journal article but shorter than a book.

SPECIAL PAPERS are surveys of research on particular topics and should be suitable for use in undergraduate courses. They may be concerned with international trade as well as international finance. They should also be of medium length.

Manuscripts should be submitted in triplicate, typed single sided and double spaced throughout on 8½ by 11 white bond paper. Publication can be expedited if manuscripts are computer keyboarded in WordPerfect 5.1 or a compatible program. Additional instructions and a style guide are available from the Section.

How to Obtain Publications

The Section's publications are distributed free of charge to college, university, and public libraries and to nongovernmental, nonprofit research institutions. Eligible institutions may ask to be placed on the Section's permanent mailing list.

Individuals and institutions not qualifying for free distribution may receive all publications for the calendar year for a subscription fee of $40.00. Late subscribers will receive all back issues for the year during which they subscribe. Subscribers should notify the Section promptly of any change in address, giving the old address as well as the new.

Publications may be ordered individually, with payment made in advance. ESSAYS and REPRINTS cost $8.00 each; STUDIES and SPECIAL PAPERS cost $11.00. An additional $1.50 should be sent for postage and handling within the United States, Canada, and Mexico; $1.75 should be added for surface delivery outside the region.

All payments must be made in U.S. dollars. Subscription fees and charges for single issues will be waived for organizations and individuals in countries where foreign-exchange regulations prohibit dollar payments.

Please address all correspondence, submissions, and orders to:

International Finance Section
Department of Economics, Fisher Hall
Princeton University
Princeton, New Jersey 08544–1021

List of Recent Publications

A complete list of publications may be obtained from the International Finance Section.

ESSAYS IN INTERNATIONAL FINANCE

163. Arminio Fraga, *German Reparations and Brazilian Debt: A Comparative Study*. (July 1986)
164. Jack M. Guttentag and Richard J. Herring, *Disaster Myopia in International Banking*. (September 1986)
165. Rudiger Dornbusch, *Inflation, Exchange Rates, and Stabilization*. (October 1986)
166. John Spraos, *IMF Conditionality: Ineffectual, Inefficient, Mistargeted*. (December 1986)
167. Rainer Stefano Masera, *An Increasing Role for the ECU: A Character in Search of a Script*. (June 1987)
168. Paul Mosley, *Conditionality as Bargaining Process: Structural-Adjustment Lending, 1980–86*. (October 1987)
169. Paul A. Volcker, Ralph C. Bryant, Leonhard Gleske, Gottfried Haberler, Alexandre Lamfalussy, Shijuro Ogata, Jesús Silva-Herzog, Ross M. Starr, James Tobin, and Robert Triffin, *International Monetary Cooperation: Essays in Honor of Henry C. Wallich*. (December 1987)
170. Shafiqul Islam, *The Dollar and the Policy-Performance-Confidence Mix*. (July 1988)
171. James M. Boughton, *The Monetary Approach to Exchange Rates: What Now Remains?* (October 1988)
172. Jack M. Guttentag and Richard M. Herring, *Accounting for Losses On Sovereign Debt: Implications for New Lending*. (May 1989)
173. Benjamin J. Cohen, *Developing-Country Debt: A Middle Way*. (May 1989)
174. Jeffrey D. Sachs, *New Approaches to the Latin American Debt Crisis*. (July 1989)
175. C. David Finch, *The IMF: The Record and the Prospect*. (September 1989)
176. Graham Bird, *Loan-Loss Provisions and Third-World Debt*. (November 1989)
177. Ronald Findlay, *The "Triangular Trade" and the Atlantic Economy of the Eighteenth Century: A Simple General-Equilibrium Model*. (March 1990)
178. Alberto Giovannini, *The Transition to European Monetary Union*. (November 1990)
179. Michael L. Mussa, *Exchange Rates in Theory and in Reality*. (December 1990)
180. Warren L. Coats, Jr., Reinhard W. Furstenberg, and Peter Isard, *The SDR System and the Issue of Resource Transfers*. (December 1990)
181. George S. Tavlas, *On the International Use of Currencies: The Case of the Deutsche Mark*. (March 1991)
182. Tommaso Padoa-Schioppa, ed., with Michael Emerson, Kumiharu Shigehara, and Richard Portes, *Europe After 1992: Three Essays*. (May 1991)
183. Michael Bruno, *High Inflation and the Nominal Anchors of an Open Economy*. (June 1991)
184. Jacques J. Polak, *The Changing Nature of IMF Conditionality*. (September 1991)

185. Ethan B. Kapstein, *Supervising International Banks: Origins and Implications of the Basle Accord.* (December 1991)
186. Alessandro Giustiniani, Francesco Papadia, and Daniela Porciani, *Growth and Catch-Up in Central and Eastern Europe: Macroeconomic Effects on Western Countries.* (April 1992)
187. Michele Fratianni, Jürgen von Hagen, and Christopher Waller, *The Maastricht Way to EMU.* (June 1992)
188. Pierre-Richard Agénor, *Parallel Currency Markets in Developing Countries: Theory, Evidence, and Policy Implications.* (November 1992)
189. Beatriz Armendariz de Aghion and John Williamson, *The G-7's Joint-and-Several Blunder.* (April 1993)
190. Paul Krugman, *What Do We Need to Know About the International Monetary System?* (July 1993)
191. Peter M. Garber and Michael G. Spencer, *The Dissolution of the Austro-Hungarian Empire: Lessons for Currency Reform.* (February 1994)
192. Raymond F. Mikesell, *The Bretton Woods Debates: A Memoir.* (March 1994)
193. Graham Bird, *Economic Assistance to Low-Income Countries: Should the Link Be Resurrected?* (July 1994)
194. Lorenzo Bini-Smaghi, Tommaso Padoa-Schioppa, and Francesco Papadia, *The Transition to EMU in the Maastricht Treaty.* (November 1994)
195. Ariel Buira, *Reflections on the International Monetary System.* (January 1995)
196. Shinji Takagi, *From Recipient to Donor: Japan's Official Aid Flows, 1945 to 1990 and Beyond.* (March 1995)
197. Patrick Conway, *Currency Proliferation: The Monetary Legacy of the Soviet Union.* (June 1995)

PRINCETON STUDIES IN INTERNATIONAL FINANCE

57. Stephen S. Golub, *The Current-Account Balance and the Dollar: 1977–78 and 1983–84.* (October 1986)
58. John T. Cuddington, *Capital Flight: Estimates, Issues, and Explanations.* (December 1986)
59. Vincent P. Crawford, *International Lending, Long-Term Credit Relationships, and Dynamic Contract Theory.* (March 1987)
60. Thorvaldur Gylfason, *Credit Policy and Economic Activity in Developing Countries with IMF Stabilization Programs.* (August 1987)
61. Stephen A. Schuker, *American "Reparations" to Germany, 1919–33: Implications for the Third-World Debt Crisis.* (July 1988)
62. Steven B. Kamin, *Devaluation, External Balance, and Macroeconomic Performance: A Look at the Numbers.* (August 1988)
63. Jacob A. Frenkel and Assaf Razin, *Spending, Taxes, and Deficits: International-Intertemporal Approach.* (December 1988)
64. Jeffrey A. Frankel, *Obstacles to International Macroeconomic Policy Coordination.* (December 1988)
65. Peter Hooper and Catherine L. Mann, *The Emergence and Persistence of the U.S. External Imbalance, 1980–87.* (October 1989)

66. Helmut Reisen, *Public Debt, External Competitiveness, and Fiscal Discipline in Developing Countries*. (November 1989)
67. Victor Argy, Warwick McKibbin, and Eric Siegloff, *Exchange-Rate Regimes for a Small Economy in a Multi-Country World*. (December 1989)
68. Mark Gersovitz and Christina H. Paxson, *The Economies of Africa and the Prices of Their Exports*. (October 1990)
69. Felipe Larraín and Andrés Velasco, *Can Swaps Solve the Debt Crisis? Lessons from the Chilean Experience*. (November 1990)
70. Kaushik Basu, *The International Debt Problem, Credit Rationing and Loan Pushing: Theory and Experience*. (October 1991)
71. Daniel Gros and Alfred Steinherr, *Economic Reform in the Soviet Union: Pas de Deux between Disintegration and Macroeconomic Destabilization*. (November 1991)
72. George M. von Furstenberg and Joseph P. Daniels, *Economic Summit Declarations, 1975–1989: Examining the Written Record of International Cooperation*. (February 1992)
73. Ishac Diwan and Dani Rodrik, *External Debt, Adjustment, and Burden Sharing: A Unified Framework*. (November 1992)
74. Barry Eichengreen, *Should the Maastricht Treaty Be Saved?* (December 1992)
75. Adam Klug, *The German Buybacks, 1932–1939: A Cure for Overhang?* (November 1993)
76. Tamim Bayoumi and Barry Eichengreen, *One Money or Many? Analyzing the Prospects for Monetary Unification in Various Parts of the World*. (September 1994)
77. Edward E. Leamer, *The Heckscher-Ohlin Model in Theory and Practice*. (February 1995)
78. Thorvaldur Gylfason, *The Macroeconomics of European Agriculture*. (May 1995)
79. Angus S. Deaton and Ronald I. Miller, *International Commodity Prices, Macroeconomic Performance, and Politics in Sub-Saharan Africa*. (December 1995)
80. Chander Kant, *Foreign Direct Investment and Capital Flight*. (April 1996)

SPECIAL PAPERS IN INTERNATIONAL ECONOMICS

16. Elhanan Helpman, *Monopolistic Competition in Trade Theory*. (June 1990)
17. Richard Pomfret, *International Trade Policy with Imperfect Competition*. (August 1992)
18. Hali J. Edison, *The Effectiveness of Central-Bank Intervention: A Survey of the Literature After 1982*. (July 1993)

REPRINTS IN INTERNATIONAL FINANCE

27. Peter B. Kenen, *Transitional Arrangements for Trade and Payments Among the CMEA Countries*; reprinted from *International Monetary Fund Staff Papers* 38 (2), 1991. (July 1991)
28. Peter B. Kenen, *Ways to Reform Exchange-Rate Arrangements*; reprinted from *Bretton Woods: Looking to the Future*, 1994. (November 1994)